POCKET SIZE COLORING BOOK FOR
ADULTS RELAXATION

MW01233934

TRAVEL SIZE COLORING

SCOTT ANISTON

While every precaution has been taken in the preparation of this book, the author and the publisher assume no responsibility for errors or omissions, or for damages resulting from the use of the information contained herein.

Pocket Size Coloring Books For Adults Relaxation
Travel Size Coloring

First Edition. August 08, 2019

Copyright © 2019 – Scott Aniston

ISBN: 9781081721565
Written by Scott Aniston

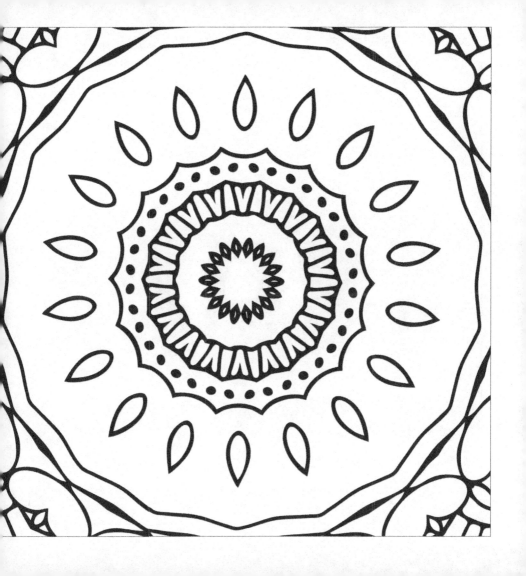

Made in the USA
Coppell, TX
27 October 2023

23448352R00049